Cont

Cover Art: *Adoration of the Christ Child* by Sassoferrato (1609-1685); Naples, Italy. Photo credit: Scala / Art resource, NY

HAIL THE HEAVEN BORN
A Study Book

Copyright © 2007 by Abingdon Press.

℗ Abingdon Press

ISBN-13: 978-0-687-49095-0

Manufactured in the United States of America

07 08 09 10 11 12 13 14 15 16—10 9 8 7 6 5 4 3 2 1

Introduction

News of the new Highway 64 had caused great commotion in the small communities of eastern North Carolina. At the time, I was living in one of those rural counties, about an hour's drive inland from the shore, where I served as pastor of three, close-knit congregations. Washington County observed different rhythms than the ones more familiar to urban dwellers. Out in the open countryside, everything seemed bigger and slower; and that wasn't a bad thing. People daily set their clocks on the sun's schedule; human bodies rising simultaneously with the great heavenly body, like musicians raising their instruments when the conductor steps before them. It took my family—all of us urbanites since birth—time to readjust to life guided more by the four seasons of the year than the fitful stops and starts so prevalent in the sleep-deprived, frenzied scramble of the city. Perhaps that is why news of a new highway, bringing traffic, noise, and "progress" to the area was so suspect.

"It is going to change everything," one farmer said. "Life as we know it will never be the same." "And don't think it will bring resources here either," a neighbor chimed in, "because they may look at our town and decide we don't even warrant an exit ramp." Listening to their hopes and fears, I became deeply aware of something that had never occurred to me before: Highway construction changes things. It changes people, communities, and even an entire way of life. One thing was clear: The highway was coming, and everyone in Washington County knew it in their bones. The question was now becoming, "How do we prepare?"

The highway metaphor works well for the church's season of Advent, and I readily admit it is not original. All three of the synoptic Gospels have John the Baptist announcing a highway, quoting words from the prophet Isaiah:

"A voice cries out: / 'In the wilderness prepare the way of the LORD, / make straight in the desert a highway for our God. / Every valley shall be lifted up, / and every mountain and hill be made low; / the uneven ground shall become level, / and the rough places a plain. / Then the glory of the LORD shall be revealed, / and all people shall see it together." (Isaiah 40:3-5)

John the Baptist announced more than a highway. He announced a coming Messiah. HAIL THE HEAVEN BORN,[1] seeks to stand with John the Baptist, Charles Wesley, and a hosts of other highway construction workers who continue to announce to the world that a Messiah is coming: Now is the time to make ready.

---

[1] From the beloved carol and hymn "Hark! The Herald Angels Sing," by Charles Wesley.

Traveling Backward Toward Bethlehem

Scriptures for Advent:
The First Sunday
Isaiah 2:1-5
Romans 13:11-14
Matthew 24:36-44

If Advent is a season of preparation, anticipation, and expectation of the coming Messiah, how should God's people make ready? The church, in her wisdom, points us to Holy Writ. Here, in the deep and fertile soil of God's Word are the tools for highway construction. Here, as we search and study the Scriptures together, we discover a means of grace where God warns, exhorts, corrects, and announces.

By December 2nd, the world around us is already saturated with signs of Christmas. We may bemoan the growing commercialization of the season that keeps backing up towards Thanksgiving, but most of us can also enjoy the familiar sights and sounds that fill the air. Local malls spray snow on winter scenes filled with festive figurines. Area businesses and community organizations throw small parties where wassail and cookies abound. Christmas music floods the airways, and strings of light adorn more and more front yards with each passing day.

The world turns our eyes toward Christmas, or at least the trappings of the holiday season. It only seems natural for Christians to turn their eyes toward Bethlehem in response. So why do the passages for the first Sunday of Advent speak nothing of shepherds watching, cattle lowing, and heavenly hosts singing? Instead, these texts have us leaping over the manger and looking ahead to Jesus' second advent where he promised to return in power and glory. The prophet Isaiah paints a dramatic picture of the future house of God where the Lord "shall judge between the nations." Paul issues an urgent appeal for people to wake up. Matthew likens the coming days to the great Flood in the days of Noah, when water caught everyone unaware.

These biblical warning signs are not placed before us to dowse seasonal festivities but to remind us that Advent is not just about waxing nostalgic at the Nativity. It is about welcoming the living Christ who lives and reigns with God the Father and the Spirit and who is coming again to judge the living and the dead. The sessions for this week serve to put us on notice that the road to Bethlehem does not stop there, and the events that take place in the City of David make little sense unless we remember the final destination on the other side of the Nativity.

STREAMING TOWARD THE MOUNTAIN
ISAIAH 2:1-5

There is an old saying: "If you do not know where you are going, any road will take you there." The prophet Isaiah may have never heard the modern expression, but the powerful and compelling image that he paints in Chapter 2 demonstrates clearly that God's people have a specific destination ahead. The next stop just around the corner is God's holy mountain.

The images Isaiah, son of Amoz, sees are nothing short of breathtaking. The call goes forth to "come, let us go up," and all the nations respond by setting out on pilgrimage toward the glorified city of Zion.

This is no sightseeing trip to God's country for casual tourists or curious travelers. This is no weekend hike in the hills to ease mounting stress and get a little exercise. This trek up the mountain is nothing less than the culmi-nation of human history. This is a peek into God's preferred future for all creation, and it is a dramatic scene that elicits joy and judgment: "They shall beat their swords into plowshares, / and their spears into pruning hooks; / nation shall not lift up sword against nation, / neither shall they learn war any more" (verse 4).

There it is again: judgment and joy. Who would not joyfully welcome weapons of war and mass destruction being transformed into common farming tools for planting and harvesting? It is a vision that seems so compelling and inviting that we often quickly dismiss it out of hand. It is a distant future that is beyond human comprehension, or it is an idealistic one that provokes thought but cannot be taken seriously in the here and now. The very prospect of such massive disarmament pronounces sentence on humanity's historical reliance on fear, war, mistrust, and violence to secure our lives and our livelihood. God's demilitarization project on the mountain condemns our warmongering, our hankering to be on top, and our trust in "might makes right." It is a cautionary road sign that causes us to stop, check the map, and make sure what road we are on and what destination it is leading us toward.

Isaiah's vision is also one that can inspire the Christian imagination and equip God's people to live into it in new and fresh ways.

I will never forget one vivid example of such prophetic imagining that took place years ago in Butner, North Carolina. The War Department made an historic decision to sell a huge military campus called Camp Butner to the state of North Carolina for the price of $1. Munitions were removed in a careful operation that required teams to locate unexploded items and carefully remove them from the training fields. The camp was then transformed into a psychiatric hospital serving 16 counties. The resulting John Umstead Hospital later adopted a logo inspired by Isaiah's vision: the image of a man holding a sword in one hand and exchanging it for a plow in the other.

Over the course of one summer, I served John Umstead Hospital as a student chaplain while I was in divinity school at Duke University. Each time I walked the halls of the former-barracks-turned-healing-station, I had a sense that Isaiah's vision was sweeping out of the future, trying desperately to grab a world resigned to living the status quo and wake it up to the transforming possibilities of God's coming kingdom. Such is the power of a vision from God. It has the ability to make people dream dreams that they would not otherwise have thought possible.

The word picture in Isaiah begins with uphill movement. The nations are streaming up to "the highest of the mountains." The call is issued for people to "go up to the mountain of the Lord" (verses 2-3). It would be easy to view all this implied climbing as a kind of works righteousness, where God's kingdom of light and peace is wholly dependent on a few able-bodied people, a few expert mountain climbers, a few hardy outdoor guides who alone can hike up this spiritual Mount Everest. Nothing could be further from the truth. Look closer at the text, and you will soon discover that there is also movement coming down the mountain: "For out of Zion shall go forth instruction, / and the word of the Lord from Jerusalem" (verse 3). God's teaching and God's word are coming down; and they descend the slopes bringing light, judgment, and peace with them.

It is God's word and God's teaching that equip those on pilgrimage toward God's house. It is the brilliant light of God's peaceable kingdom that illuminates the path of the nations and allows people to avoid the rocks and slippery places. It is the very city of Zion that peeks over the horizon, its sheer size and brilliance drawing all nations and all peoples into its marvelous light; spurring fellow sojourners on to love and good deeds; strengthening weary travelers to look up from the road and see where they are headed; inspiring the disillusioned pilgrim to keep putting one foot in front of the other, knowing that an awesome destination in God is just around the corner.

Can you see what Isaiah sees? Can you imagine nations streaming toward God's holy mountain? Perhaps our vision is too clouded with the sight of morning rush-hour traffic streaming to work or hoards of people flocking to the malls every weekend. The prophet Isaiah challenges all of us who are walking, driving, hiking, and rushing around to take a moment and stop. Examine where we are and where we are headed. Take spiritual inventory of where we have been and what road we have chosen. If it is not the road to God's house on the mountain, then it may be time for us to make a U-turn.

What road are you traveling on? Do you know where you are headed?

Reflect a moment on the sword into plowshare image. How can you allow Isaiah's vision to challenge and transform the way you relate to others? In what ways have you succumbed to skepticism and resignation to "the way things are" rather than opening yourself to God's in-breaking kingdom of peace, light, and love?

THE ALARM CLOCK IS RINGING
ROMANS 13:11-14

I have a problem getting up the first time my alarm clock goes off in the morning. The truth is, I am not a morning person. The irony is that I married one. My wife leaps out of bed every morning cheerful and ready to brew a hot cup of java. I, on the other hand, engage in hand-to-sound combat with the snooze button for as long as my nerves can take it. I am convinced that God brought my wife and me together almost 20 years ago, which is one of the many reasons I have concluded that God has a sense of humor.

As I read this passage from Romans, I cannot help but think of my alarm clock. Imagine an alarm clock having a different wake-up sound during the season of Advent, one inspired by this passage from Romans. Instead of waking to an annoying buzzer or the sound of holiday music coursing over the airwaves, one hears these words coming from the bedside tabletop: "You know what time it is! It is time for you to wake up! Salvation is nearer to you now than when you first became a believer. The night is far gone, the day is near. Get up! Lay aside the works of darkness, and put on the armor of light." There is something about the content of the message that demands attention. It is a message that cannot be easily dismissed by rolling over and burying one's head under the covers.

Chapter 13 gives us another disconcerting Advent text that rivets our attention on the second coming of Christ and the need for watchfulness and readiness. The urgency is readily apparent. The image of waking from slumber is poignant and rich in meaning for

Christian believers. Just like predawn, the moment that lies between the complete darkness of night and the full light of the risen sun, Christians are living in an "in-between moment" in salvation history. Light, God's light, has come into the world through a long-awaited Messiah. Through Jesus' birth, life, death, and resurrection, this light has entered the world, dispelling the darkness of sin, disobedience, and death. Yet there are still deeds done in darkness and living that seeks to flee the coming light.

For all those who are not early risers, Paul sends out a wake up call. In 2002, astronomers and stargazers drew people's attention to the heavens. The focus was on one particular celestial body that was making rare and glorious appearances just before each sunrise. It was the planet Venus. One article stated, "Venus dominates predawn sky all winter." The writer went on to talk about this new, radiant companion rising in the eastern sky, a presence that was welcome company to anyone who could manage to get up early enough to witness it. The phenomenon lasted well into the first half of 2003.

Thinking back on that time, I wonder how many people missed the pre-dawn Venus. I seem to recall some talk about it but can honestly say I do not remember rising in time to see what all the fuss was about. As far as I, and perhaps all other early-morning cur-mudgeons were concerned, it was a non-event, not because it was not happening on a daily basis but because I was not paying it any attention. I am sure that nothing about my apathy changed the brightness or regularity of the Venus sky. I was simply slumbering, oblivious to this celestial body that was inspiring the world and causing people to readjust their schedules, set their clocks, and change their behavior, all so they could be awake when the planet reached its zenith. How many are slumbering in this pre-dawn light of Christ's second coming? In a spiritual sense, apathy is slumber.

Paul lets us know that slumber can be dangerous, especially when it refers to those who are asleep in the wee hours of salvation history, somewhere between the appearance of the Bethlehem star and the dawn of the risen Son. On that day, there will be a celestial body that appears, not to dominate the sky but to inaugurate a new day when every knee will bow and every tongue confess that Jesus Christ is Lord (Philippians 2:10-11). The alarm clock is ringing, and "the day is near" (Romans 13:12). Now is the time to wake up. To those who hear the alarm, the question then becomes, What does one do next? Paul exhorts us to get up and get dressed, to "put on the armor of light; . . . put on the Lord Jesus Christ" (verses 12, 14).

In the early church, baptismal candidates participated in a liturgy that took this image of dressing seriously. The person to be baptized would strip completely before entering what was often a tomb-shaped font. Nothing alien was allowed to go down into the waters. Each person came to baptism naked as the day they were born. After coming up from the water, a deacon or deaconess would then wrap the person in a white robe or a cloth symbolizing how they had "put on Christ." The newly baptized Christian was then lead down a corridor to a worship gathering where they could participate in their first Eucharist.

Remembering our own holy baptism is an important part of our pre-dawn preparations. In baptism, we are called to die to all the "works of darkness ... reveling and drunkenness, ... debauchery and licentiousness, ... quarreling and jealously" (verses 12-13) mentioned in Romans. In baptism, we are called to rise to new life in Jesus just as we await his return; and we are called to remember who we are and whose we are— namely, a sojourning people who have been called out of darkness into God's marvelous light.

Wake up. Put off the works of darkness. While the world would have us scrounging through the attic to find that "Peace on Earth" plaque for the front door decorations, war on earth is killing and maiming sisters and brothers around the world. *Wake up. Put off the works of darkness.* While the world is partying like there is no tomorrow, the church is called to put on Christ

and come dressed for a great banquet feast that is being prepared for God's faithful. *Wake up. Put off the works of darkness.* Some in the church may mistakenly think there is not much to worry about with regard to reveling, drunkenness, debauchery, and licentiousness. The last two works mentioned, quarreling and jealousy, are more readily apparent in our common life together. One does not have to be a charter member of the community of faith to experience quarreling and jealousy among people who are supposed to embody God's love and forgiveness. *Wake up. Put off the works of darkness.* A new world is dawning. This is one time that the alarm clock should be heeded.

In what ways do you need to wake up and heed this urgent appeal in Romans?

What things in your life cause you to slumber and ignore the coming sunrise?

In a world that seems consigned to darkness, how can you witness to a different reality?

THE THIEF IS COMING TO TOWN
MATTHEW 24:36-44

Few people realize how radical and countercultural Advent can be until they start to pay attention to what the church is busy reading on the Sundays prior to Christmas. If the prophet Isaiah and Paul's letter to the Romans were not enough to interrupt our holiday business as usual, the Gospel of Matthew should do the trick in this striking apocalyptic passage from Chapter 24. While we hear "Santa Claus Is Coming to Town" on the radio, Matthew 24 compares the coming of the Lord to a thief in the night! No, this is not the Grinch that stole Christmas. No, this is not a cutesy, full-length animated feature film for the kids to watch while there is a warm fire in the hearth. This is the stuff of the real Christmas; the news of a God who more closely resembles a burglar than a fat jolly man in a red suit.

Jesus as a thief. It is not exactly the Christmas card caption that one would expect to find when looking for something to mail to family and friends. In Matthew, this image is one of four examples of the imminent return of Christ. Each of the images describe people who are caught unprepared for Christ's coming, preoccupied as they are with work, relationships, and everyday living. Jesus' return is like the flood in the time of Noah that swept down on people who "knew nothing until the flood came and swept them away" (verse 39). A second image has two people in a field, presumably just clocking in for a regular day's labor; one is taken, and the other is left behind. Still a third image is again in the workplace where two women are "grinding meal together"; one is taken and another left. Finally, we are told that Jesus is like a thief who breaks into the house while the owner is sleeping.

The thief metaphor has much to commend it. If Jesus is a thief, he is one who has his eye on more than just the loose change in the house. This thief is coming for the whole world—lock, stock, and barrel. Of course, this particular burglar is not really stealing, since the "earth is the LORD's and all that is in it" (Psalm 24:1); but human beings have spent thousands of years convincing themselves otherwise. The imminent return of the Son of Man in thief-like fashion may be welcomed by those who have stayed awake in watchful readiness, but it is likely to be greeted as an intrusion to others who are suffering spiritual amnesia about the true owner of the house. The other frustrating thing about thieves is that they refuse to schedule their nighttime visits on a daily planner. We live in a world that marks time down to the millisecond. If it is not in the personal calendar or PDA, it is not going to happen; or so we think.

Matthew shocks us out of this illusion of control with words that reveal our ignorance and inability to govern God's future: "But about that day and hour no one knows, neither the angels of heaven, nor the Son, but only the Father" (Matthew 24:36). One thing is certain: Jesus is coming again. What is equally certain is that no one can be certain about when. No one.

There are some who read these passages in Matthew and choose to focus on only one aspect of the text—"left behind." The famous series by Tim LaHaye has captivated many who have become obsessed by images of the rapture. Who has not seen the car bumper sticker in front of them at one time or another: "In case of rapture, this car will be unmanned." Some people respond to this kind of interpretation with anxiety.

I will never forget a friend of mine who vividly recalled watching many of the rapture-type films during his years as a teenager. He had been part of a youth group where the threat of hell always seemed to get more airtime than the promise of heaven, and it had always left him more than a little nervous. He recalled a visit to his grandmother's home one week. He came indoors from playing outside and went in the kitchen to say "hi" to his grandmother. There was food cooking on the stove, water running at the sink, and no one in sight. He called and called and made a cursory search of the premises to no avail. His first thought? Rapture! He was convinced the rapture had happened because his grandma was the best Christian he had ever met. If anyone was going first, it was Grandma!

The passage in Matthew's Gospel is not there to generate anxiety but watchfulness: "Keep awake therefore, for you do not know on what day your Lord is coming" (verse 42). It was precisely this type of watchfulness John Wesley had in mind when he gathered early Methodists into societies and classes. These small groups gathered "to watch over one another in love, that they might help each other to work out their salvation."[1] Everyone who entered into this covenant together agreed to do no harm, avoiding evil of every kind; do good, of every possible sort as often as possible to as many people as possible; and to participate in the means of grace that included regular attendance in worship, the ministry of the Word (read or expounded), participating in the Lord's Supper as often as possible, family and private prayer, Bible study (searching the Scriptures), and fasting or abstinence.

Preparation for Christ's second advent is not a matter of passing interest or just another interesting topic for theological discussion. It is a way of life that demands people stay awake and not allow themselves to drift into the sleepiness of apathy, inattention, disobedience, and rebellion. In Matthew's Gospel, Jesus says that the Son of Man will come again like a thief in the night and that no one knows the day or time. To prepare ourselves, we can pray for one another, hold one another accountable, and occasionally grab the shoulder or arm of a sister or a brother in Christ long enough to keep spiritual slumber from overtaking them. If we are to be ready when the thief comes to town, we must learn to be more intentional about watching over one another in love. We must remain vigilant in our love and service to God and neighbor. We must regularly engage in holy habits of heart and life, participating in the very means of grace that sharpen our senses and keep our spiritual nerve-endings alert and vigilant.

Take a moment to write a list of practices or habits that serve to keep you watchful. Which ones do you participate in regularly? Which ones are less frequent or absent in your discipleship?

What are concrete things you can do this Advent season to become more vigilant and watchful?

[1] From "The General Rules" in *The Book of Discipline of The United Methodist Church, 2004.*

O Christmas Tree, O Christmas Tree

Scriptures for Advent:
The Second Sunday
Isaiah 11:1-10
Romans 15:4-13
Matthew 3:1-12

I love the sights and sounds of Christmas as much as the next person; and one of my favorite family traditions is the annual pilgrimage to find a tree, place strings of light upon it, and decorate it with ornaments from previous years. It was only later that I learned of pagan origins of this tradition and how it was adapted by Christians. Though some who have learned of this history have decided to chunk the tree tradition, I have always thought that was a bit of an overreaction. I believe that my children can "deck the halls" and the Christmas tree and still learn the true meaning of Christmas.

There are other trees to learn about during Advent and Christmas. Many churches include a Chrismon tree in their decorations. *Chrismon,* a word combining the word *Christ* with *monogram,* stands for the monograms or symbols of Christ that are placed on the tree to celebrate Jesus as Savior and Incarnate Lord. Another Advent tree tradition is the Jesse tree, which is a bit different and is described in more detail below.

So why all this talk about trees on the second Sunday of Advent? In part, it is because trees keep showing up in our Scripture passages for the day. The prophet Isaiah spoke of a shoot coming out from the stump of Jesse and a branch growing out of his roots (Isaiah 11:1). Here is a tree tradition that reminds us of Jesus' Jewishness. Jesus did not just drop down out of nowhere. It is scandalous for some to think that Jesus had parents, grandparents, and great-grandparents; but the true mystery of the Incarnation can not be grasped without realizing Christ's full divinity and full humanity, which is so passionately expressed in the words of the second stanza of Charles Wesley's hymn "Hark the Herald Angels Sing": "Veiled in flesh the Godhead see; / hail th'incarnate Deity / pleased as man with man to dwell / Jesus, our Emmanuel."

The Epistle passage from Romans returns to this family tree image as Paul writes, "The root of Jesse shall come, / the one who rises to rule the Gentiles; / in him the Gentiles shall hope" (Romans 15:12). Evidently, this is one family tree that grows more by baptism than by biology; and it keeps including more people in its branches.

Finally, we travel to the desert to hear a word from John the Baptist, and the subject of trees comes up again: "Even now the ax is lying at the root of the trees, every tree therefore that does not bear good fruit is cut down and thrown into the fire" (Matthew 3:10).

"O Christmas Tree, O Christmas Tree." The famous German carol may have us thinking of ornaments, evergreens, and annual family traditions; but the Scripture passages for the second Sunday of Advent have other trees in mind. They all seem to foreshadow and point us toward another more important tree that would be crowned with the Son of David, suspended between heaven and earth. It is on that tree, adorned with the Son of the living God, that Jesus would die for the sins of the whole world.

A CHRISTMAS TREE
WITH ROOTS
ISAIAH 11:1-10

Jesus had roots. If any contemporary Christian has a tendency to forget that simple yet profound truth, this passage from Isaiah should serve as a poignant reminder. When the church celebrates Pentecost, many people like to refer to it as the "birthday" of the church. Acts 2 certainly describes something new and exciting taking place when the great multitude gathered in Jerusalem; but in all the exuberance and celebration, one should not dismiss the specifically Jewish nature of the assembly: "Devout Jews from every nation under heaven" (Acts 2:5). Unfortunately, it has become too easy to forget Jesus was a Jew who had grandparents, ancestors, and a family tree.

One Advent season tradition that makes this same point is the Jesse tree. As early as the 11th century, Jesse trees began to appear in Christian art and writings and can now be found in many manuscripts, wood carvings, stone etchings, stained glass windows, and Orthodox iconography. Many of these artistic depictions have Jesse, the father of King David, reclining with a branch springing up out of his body. On the branches above him one can often see prophets, kings, and patriarchs from the Scriptures. Near the top of the tree is usually Mary, the mother of Jesus, with her son at the apex. Two of the more famous depictions of a Jesse tree can be found in modern-day France. One is an ivory panel on display at the Louvre Museum, and the other is a magnificent stained-glass window at the Chartres Cathedral that dates back to the 12th century.

Jesse trees are now a regular Advent tradition in many churches. Sometimes created on banners or on a real tree, churches will adorn the Jesse tree with a different ornament every day of Advent until Christmas. The ornaments represent different symbols or people in the Old Testament and often have a Scripture accompanying their placement on the tree. An ornament depicting a tree with fruit might accompany a reading from Genesis 2. A rainbow might be placed on the tree while reading of Noah and the ark. A ram might allude to the time when Abraham offered Isaac on the mountain. Jesse trees are one way that the church can tell the story of Jesus from Creation to Incarnation. It is an attempt to remind us of Jesus' roots.

The inspiration for Jesse trees most likely came from Isaiah: "A shoot shall come out from the stump of Jesse, / and a branch shall grow out of his roots" (Isaiah 11:1). Jesus did not just appear out of nowhere. This Jesus is not only the one about whom the angels sang but the one of whom the prophets foretold. Isaiah may have never comprehended the full significance of his words, but this poetic pronouncement in Chapter 11 is a powerful foreshadowing of a time not far in the future when "the Lord will extend his hand yet a second time" (verse 11), when a descendent of

Jesse will ascend the throne of David, coming with "wisdom and understanding ... / counsel and might, ... / knowledge and the fear of the LORD" (verse 2). The message is clear. A king is coming and not just any king. This is a king that comes from a royal bloodline that can be traced all the way back to Jesse and his son David.

The reign of this promised king is different than all the kings and kingdoms. This is a king that does not have to rely on the five senses; senses that can often lead to erroneous conclusions or a rush to judgment. No, this king "shall not judge by what his eyes see, / or decide by what his ears hear; / but with righteousness he shall judge the poor, / and decide with equity for the meek of the earth" (verses 3-4). A new reign of righteousness and peace is coming, and words cannot easily capture its scope or magnificence.

Words may never fully capture the fullness of this reign spoken of by the prophet, but Isaiah's words certainly do try. This chapter in Isaiah is one of the most beloved and awe-inspiring in Scripture. The images are vivid and striking: wolves with lambs, leopards with kids, calves with lions, cows with bears, and all of these animals in the upstairs nursery with the baby. It is almost like watching *Wild Kingdom* but with a radical and unexpected twist: Prey and predator are at peace.

Last year, the world was shocked when Steve Irwin, known more widely as the "Crocodile Hunter," was killed while shooting one of his animal shows that air regularly on cable TV. For years, this animal enthusiast and conservationist had entertained thousands with his crazy antics and seemingly fearless bravado that took him to every corner of the known world and face to face with dangerous reptiles. His death was sudden and unexpected as he was barbed by a large stingray off the coast of Australia. Many commentators and observers commented that Steve died doing what he loved; but in the end, nature did what comes natural.

Yet contrary to popular opinion, the Bible suggests something quite different. Namely, that it is not natural for stingrays to attack people, for wolves to hunt lambs, or for lions to eat calves. A close reading of Genesis 1 indicates that God initially gave humans and animals "green plants" for food, not each other (Genesis 1:29-30). In other words, wild kingdom, survival of the fittest, and the "dog-eat-dog" mentality of the world was never God's original intention for creation. All the blood and mayhem shows up in Genesis 3, after the man and the woman disobeyed God. Things have been a mess ever since.

The fall affected all of creation; but Isaiah points to a coming reign when peace and tranquility will be restored, predator and prey will lie down together, and wild kingdom shall become the peaceable king-dom: "And a little child shall lead them" (Isaiah 11:6). It is an incredible image—a child leading animals that were formerly carnivores with sharp teeth, deadly claws, and menacing appetites. Years later, after the prophet first penned these words, a little child would come into the world and inaugurate a new beginning for all of creation. Ironically enough, this vulnerable and helpless child would grow into a man who would also be called the Lamb of God and the Lion of Judah. It is in that Jewish child that the hope of the world and the promise of a peaceable kingdom will be fulfilled.

Why do you think it is important to remember Jesus' lineage and family tree?

What implications do you see for contemporary Christian/Jewish dialogue and understanding?

If nature and creation is fallen, how does that challenge what you consider to be "natural" ways of relating and living?

CLOSED DOORS, CLOSED INNS, CLOSED HEARTS? ROMANS 15:4-13

Churches like to use signs and marquee slogans that communicate that all are welcome. Many people, especially immigrants, travelers, and ethnic minorities, often read such slogans as code for some are welcome: "You are welcome on our terms, with our conditions, our music, our language, and our local customs." In other words, "conform to the way we think and do things here, and we will be happy to have you sit in one of our undesignated pews each Sunday and put a little something in the offering plate." Unfortunately, this is too often an accurate description of what lies within the church walls for the unsuspecting first-time visitor.

In contrast, hear Paul's words to the Christians in Rome: "Welcome one another, therefore, just as Christ has welcomed you, for the glory of God" (Romans 15:7). This powerful, missional mandate serves as a nice summary of Chapters 14–15 in Romans. Throughout these two chapters, Paul makes it clear that the church is called to the ministry of hospitality. We are to "welcome those who are weak in faith" (14:1), to "pursue what makes for peace and for mutual upbuilding" (14:19), and to "please our neighbor for the good purpose of building up the neighbor" (15:2).

Practices of welcome and hospitality have a long, rich history among the people of Israel and the early church.[1] It seems to me, however, that many of today's welcome mats have been rolled up and stored away for good keeping. Some people may dust them off and partially roll them out this time of year for the holidays, not unlike holiday specials, as a "a limited offer for a limited time." When the season is over, we quickly roll them back up and tuck them away with the other decorations that go back into the attic.

Of course we have good reasons for putting them up. If the church rolls out the welcome mat too far, so the reasoning goes, anyone might come. If we open our homes up too much, we might run the risk of being used or abused. If we seek to live and practice radical, biblical hospitality, we might find ourselves vulnerable, uncomfortable, and unprepared for the possible repercussions. Paul wrote, "Welcome one another ... just as Christ has welcomed you" (15:7); and we are compelled to respond, "Yes, but...." Yes, but not if it means undue risk. Yes, but not if it is inconvenient. Yes, but not if it stretches our resources too far. Yes, but not if there is legal liability. Yes, but ... [fill in the blank].

Despite our reservations, the welcome mat in Romans extends longer and further than most would expect; and it is one that remains out all year long. Christ became a "servant of the circumcised" (verse 8) so that he could not only fulfill the promises made to Israel but also so that the "Gentiles might glorify God for his mercy" (verse 9). Jews and Gentiles glorifying God together; circumcised insiders welcoming uncircumcised outsiders; people receiving one another because they have been recipients of God's welcome in and through Jesus Christ! This is definitely not business as usual. This is a charge and a call to throw open the doors and to make room at the table.

One Advent tradition that brings the issue of hospitality to the forefront is the Mexican celebration of Las Posadas. The word *posada* means "shelter." For years, my bilingual congregation has celebrated our own version of Las Posadas. Though details may vary depending on the region and local customs, this Mexican tradition usually begins nine days before Christmas Eve, on December 16th, nine days symbolically representing Mary's nine months of pregnancy. Each evening, people will travel by candlelight from home to home in a given neighborhood seeking *posada* just like the Holy Family did on that first Christmas Eve. After several failed attempts at welcome at the first two homes, finally a home (the one scheduled to host the *posada* for that evening) allows the pilgrims to enter and a fiesta follows.

The liturgy that guides the dialogue at the door of each home is actually a song that is chanted back and forth. The insiders represent the innkeeper and his family. The outsiders represent Joseph and Mary. The song imagines how the exchange between these two families might have gone that first Christmas Eve. Perhaps it might also serve us to examine it here in light of Paul's call to "welcome one another." The following is an English translation of "Para Pedir Posada" ("To Ask for Lodging") with reflections I have added after each exchange:

Outside
In the name of heaven
We ask you for *posada* (shelter),
For my beloved wife
Cannot walk further.

Inside
This is not an inn.
Continue on your way
Because I can't open up.
For all I know, you could be a
  scoundrel.

Here is a homeless family looking for welcome, for shelter, and for a place to rest from traveling. The Holy Family is not alone. How many families today remain homeless in our own towns, cities, and neighborhoods? Yet the first order of business, even for an innkeeper, is assessing the risk. These verses capture well our human resistance to welcoming the stranger. We quickly make assumptions. It is safer to keep the door closed, the inn locked, and rest a reassuring hand on our wallet or purse. It is better to be safe than sorry, or so we think.

Outside
We've come from Nazareth,
And we're tired and weary.
I am a carpenter
Named José.

Inside
I could care less about your name.
Leave me alone, and let me sleep
As I already told you,
We are not opening.

Outside
We only ask for *posada*
respectfully, Señor landlord.
Only for tonight
For the queen of heaven.

Inside
If it is a queen
Who requests a place to sleep,
How is it that you are out here at
    night
Walking all by yourselves?

Everybody has a story. No doubt
the families knocking at the doors
of our local shelters have one, too;
but the time is inconvenient. The
plight of such people has nothing
to do with the people sleeping com-
fortably inside. Disturbing sleep is
akin to disturbing the peace, and
most can agree it is unpleasant and
disrespectful. Like the innkeeper,
we like to do our charity work when
we are in the mood and during
business hours only.

Outside
My wife is María.
She is the Queen of Heaven.
She is going to be the mother
Of the Divine Word.

Inside
You are José?
Your wife is María?
Enter pilgrims.
We didn't recognize you.

Outsiders and Insiders Together
Enter holy pilgrims; pilgrims
    Receive this place,
Not just our poor accommodations
But our hearts as well.

At the close of the *posada* song,
the innkeeper welcomes the pilgrims into the house and all sing
together in unison. The closing
line captures what had been at
stake throughout this encounter. It
is not about the no-vacancy signs,
inn regulations, or after-hours
policies. It is a matter of the heart.
Are you willing to open yourself up
to others? Are you willing to risk
being vulnerable?

On the other hand, what about
the people who are outside the
doors of our homes and our
churches, knocking and seeking
entry? In truth, it is often not that
obvious. We may not have anyone
beating down the door desperately
seeking entrance; but there are
certainly plenty of people who are
traveling outside who are seeking a
kind word, a warm smile, and an
invitation to friendship.

Are you willing to welcome
others the way Christ has welcomed you? If so, a whole new
understanding of Jesus' advent
awaits; one where Jew and Gen-
tile, rich and poor, homeowner
and the homeless enter together
singing and praising and filled
"with all joy and peace in believing, so that [we] may abound in
hope by the power of the Spirit"
(verse 13).

How do you open your heart
and doors to the neighbor, the
outsider, the stranger?

How might you respond when
faced with insecurities about opening the doors to our neighbors?

JOHN'S CHRISTMAS SERMON
MATTHEW 3:1-12

Every holiday season has its detractors, and the Christmas season has more than most. For every person that loves Christmas, there seems to be another person who cannot stand it. We have even popularized some of these Christmas curmudgeons so that they are regular icons of the season. Who has not heard of the unhappy Dr. Seuss character the Grinch, who cannot wait to steal Christmas and spoil everyone's holiday spirit? Mr. Scrooge is another, a man who pinched pennies and pinched the families who had few pennies to spare. During the season we may hear a malcontent who is determined to pour cold water on the warm hearth of friendship, peace, joy, and goodwill to all. It is almost as if Christmas would not be Christmas without the standard "meanies" who are rude, cranky, and downright disagreeable.

Then, as if in cahoots with this long line of killjoys, we read this Gospel passage from Matthew and hear these words: "You brood of vipers! Who warned you to flee from the wrath to come? Even now the axe is lying at the root of the trees; every tree therefore that does not bear good fruit is cut down and thrown into the fire" (Matthew 3:7, 10). How is that for a Sunday morning message of uplift, inspiration, hope, and spiritual renewal? John's wilderness sermon has a little fire and brimstone in it. Not exactly the kind of thing that looks good on the annual Christmas letter. Not too many Christmas carols use this passage from Matthew 3 as their inspiration. We want to hear about angels singing, not vipers slithering; about shepherds keeping watch over their flocks, not trees crashing to the ground and being turned into ashes. John even goes so far as to tell the multitudes that rocks have more of a future than they do unless they repent and bear fruits worthy of repentance (verse 9).

However, a closer look reveals that John is not just being cranky or rude. Unlike the Grinch or Mr. Scrooge, John was not simply looking for an opportunity to express his sour mood to those around him. Much more is at stake here, and we cannot fully understand Christmas and the coming Messiah until we have an idea about what John was up to in this sermon in the wilderness.

On the one hand, we have traditional images of the Advent season that we associate with the coming celebration of Christmas; and, on the other hand, we have John's disturbing images. Scenes of the Nativity in our homes, on our mantles, and on our lawns, complete with serene images of Joseph, Mary, and their newborn child lying in a manger, contrast with John's images of "one who is more Powerful" with a winnowing fork in hand, working up a sweat on the threshing floor of the granary, busy separating wheat from chaff (verses 11-12). Scenes of carolers traveling from home to home singing "We Wish You a Merry Christmas," " Deck the Halls," and "Joy to the World" differ markedly from John's image of sinners traveling to the desert confessing their sins and being baptized in the Jordan River. Images of a jolly man in a red suit with white trim, a big black belt, a shiny buckle, and a hearty laugh who will come to eat cookies and drink milk and leave behind a room full of gifts and special treats contrast mightily with the image of John in the wilderness, a wild-looking man dressed in camel's hair clothing and a leather belt, who eats locusts and honey and preaches sharply about the need to repent.

Why is it important to read John's Christmas sermon from the wilderness during Advent? Because John reminds us that the Babe lying in a manger is also the "Righteous Judge" who comes to separate wheat from chaff. In the word of Czeslaw Milosz the famous Polish poet and writer,

"Religion, opium for the people. To those suffering pain, humiliation, illness, and serfdom, it promised a reward in an afterlife. And now we are witnessing a transformation. A true opium for the people is a belief in nothingness after death—the huge solace of thinking that for our betrayals, greed, cowardice, murder we are not going to be judged."[2]

Milosz reminds us of why we need John's Christmas sermon from the desert. It is precisely because John corrects and reorders our distorted images of Jesus and Christmas. John reminds us that Christian faith is not an opiate for the people; the true opiate is the spiritually-numbing drug of apathy and indifference to the world's pain and suffering.

John's desert sermon cries out that more is expected of us this Christmas. "Repent, for the kingdom of heaven has come near" (Matthew 3:2). The oddly dressed preacher is calling us to turn from our ways of death so that we may embrace the gospel of life. John reminds us that Jesus did not just come to be a perpetual infant that we memorialize and place on a mantle; but he comes as our King and our Judge with a winnowing fork in hand, administering a baptism of the Holy Spirit and fire. John shakes us from our nostalgia for the Holy Family at manger-side and reminds us that we need to have a burning in our bones for millions of other poor families that still have no place for their children to sleep and eat safely.

Yes, we need a Christmas sermon like John's because it is a word that cuts to the heart, strips away all the commercialization and extra holiday baggage, and gets down to the heart of the matter. Johns tells us that we cannot just go through the motions of another Christmas. Not this year. Not next year. Not ever. God will not have it. Jesus will not stand for it. What then should we do? What response should we have to John's prophetic word from the wilderness? The sermon is clear: "Bear fruit worthy of repentance" (Matthew 3:8).

What family traditions do you observe during Advent and Christmas?

How does John's sermon challenge you to see the incarnation differently?

How will you respond to the prophet's call to repent and bear fruits worthy of repentance?

---

[1] For a full and rich understanding of the ministry of Christian hospitality, see *Making Room: Recovering Hospitality as a Christian Tradition*, by Christine D. Poh. (William B. Eerdmans Publishing Co., 1999).

[2] From "Discreet Charm of Nihilism," by Milosz Czeslaw in *The New York Review of Books* (November 19, 1998).

Do You See What I See?

Scriptures for Advent:
The Third Sunday
Isaiah 35:1-10
James 5:7-10
Matthew 11:2-11

A well-known Christmas song entitled "Do You Hear What I Hear?" begins with the words, "Said the night wind to the little lamb / Do you see what I see?" The song celebrates the traditional Nativity with its star, its song, and the birth of the Child who will bring goodness and light. In spite of the joy of this song, many struggle with the questions of God's presence.

Where is God? People wrestle with this fundamental question at one time or another. Can you see God? Can you hear God? Most people respond to such questions with a resounding no. Yet people continue to search. People continue to hope. Deep down, most people want to believe in something. They want to think that there is more to life than what they know. They secretly hope that life is more than a series of random events— some good, some bad, and some indifferent. People are looking, seeking, and hoping that someone or something can help make sense out of everything else in their lives.

People seek that missing something more during December than any other time of the year. Church attendance goes up during the Christmas season; and something about Christmas attracts otherwise non-religious people, perhaps because the season stimulates thought about deeper, spiritual things, about hidden longings, and about suppressed hopes. An annual ritual of seasonal sights and sounds promises something better; but after all the Christmas wrapping paper has been placed in the overstuffed trash bin and taken to the curb, have the people's needs and hopes been fulfilled?

What are the sights and sounds of Christmas that seem to prompt so many yearnings and longings within us? Radio stations begin to play special music that speaks of love and peace. Malls and shops pull out all the stops with elaborate, decorative displays of red, white, and green. Homes throughout each neighborhood begin to light up the night with strings of lights and festive figurines. People come to work in Santa hats or red stockings. Friends and families begin to give and receive news and cards in the mail like no other time of the year. Homeless shelters, food banks, and other non-profit organizations begin to receive more donations and offers for assistance than any other time of the year.

Such sights, sounds, and generosity are common during the weeks before Christmas. However, it seems that even before sunset on the 25th, most of the magic is gone. All too soon, life moves back to old routines. The credit card bills begin to accumulate in the mailbox. The trash can fills with paper, soon followed by the toys that did not survive the week. Students return to school. Employees return to work. With the return to our regular schedules comes a equally predictable turn to our old habits. We feel a familiar emptiness that gnaws at our consciousness and seems to whisper in our ears that Christmas is over and once again it did not touch us in a way that lasts more than three or four weeks. The seeking continues. The search for God, for meaning, for hope, for anything beyond or above what we know continues.

It is almost as if Christmas does not happen, at least not for some people. What is Christmas? What is it we expect? What is it we are supposed to look for? Why do we never seem to find it? These are the questions that this Sunday's Scriptures give answer to. Each passage seems to suggest that we have been "looking for Christmas in all the wrong places." What are the true "sights and sounds of Christmas"? Isaiah tells us to look to nature and see the deserts blossom and dry places fill with water. James reminds us to wait for the signs like a farmer waits for a precious crop from the earth. Matthew speaks of what people see and hear with the coming of Jesus. Do you hear what I hear? Do you see what I see? Hold on to your hat and get ready for a multi-sensory immersion in some amazing Advent texts.

HOME FOR THE HOLIDAYS
ISAIAH 35:1-10

A pilgrimage is a long journey that has great spiritual significance. People of virtually all religions share an idea of the holy pilgrimage where devoted followers journey to scared sites or places of special significance to their faith. Buddhists recognize at such sacred sites, all related to Buddha's life and teachings. Every able-bodied Muslim is taught to attempt at least one pilgrimage to Mecca, the holiest site in the Muslim world, during their lifetime. In first-century Judaism, Jews were required to make pilgrimage to Jerusalem at least three times a year for the Feast of Passover, the Feast of

Weeks, and Feast of Booths (Exodus 34:22). Christianity also has its share of pilgrims who have made their way to biblical landmarks and places of special significance in the lives of Jesus and Paul.

Yet today's text from Isaiah speaks of a different kind of pilgrimage. It is a journey that had been anticipated for generations of God's people but one that never seemed to come to pass. For years it had been an unrealized hope, an impossible prospect, a kind of pipe dream that seemed to grow fainter and less likely with each passing day and season. The difference with this pilgrimage is that the prophet Isaiah did not describe pilgrims traveling far from home to sacred destinations in distant lands; in fact, it was quite the opposite. This story tells of pilgrims—in this case exiles— traveling from a distant destination to the one place that had become the subject of their prayers, their songs, their conversations, and their aspirations for the future. They were traveling home.

And what a homecoming the poet describes! This is the stuff of fiesta, celebration, joy, and hope. The return expedition is full of arresting images: "The wilderness and the dry land will be glad / the desert shall rejoice and blossom; / . . . with joy and singing" (35:1-2). The last time the people of Israel traveled to freedom through a desert was in their exodus from Egypt. That first exodus was fraught with hardship and obstacles; it was a journey marked by disobedience, thirst, hunger, God's provision, Israel's forgetfulness, and 40 years of asking for directions. This time, the exodus road from Babylon to Zion was adorned with flowers (verse 2). The parched earth and dry sand became pools of water and springs of life (verse 7). The very path for the journey itself had been consecrated and blessed! (verses 8-9).

This journey is also different from other religious pilgrimages in another way. As odd and mysterious as it may sound, for this pilgrimage, the point of departure, the journey itself, and the final destination are all the same. God is the beginning, middle, and end. In other words, this journey says more about the God who delivers captives than the people who have experienced captivity. It says more about the God who prepared a holy highway in the wilderness than it does about the hardy pilgrims who set out from Babylon. It says more about the God who calls Israel to return to their home in God than it does about the traveler's desire to locate earthly dwellings where one can sleep, eat, and hang their hat.

The Advent and Christmas seasons offer several stories about traveling. We read about Mary and Joseph taking that first Christmas trip where they experienced the Roman Empire's version of April 15. We hear about shepherds jogging over from a nearby field to visit a makeshift maternity ward and a peasant family about to give birth. We read of Magi making a two-year trek into the unknown simply because they saw a star and believed a prophecy. And here in Isaiah we read about God's people making their way home after years of exile in a foreign land.

Each year, the holiday season is full of contemporary journeys as well. We climb on commercial airlines or interstate freeways to see loved ones for Christmas or New Year's. Even when we are prevented from making an annual pilgrimage to see family and friends, we often have such destinations in our thoughts during the season, humming versions of "I'll be home for Christmas, if only in my dreams."

For good for or ill, Christmas has become synonymous with "family Christmas." Extended families often gather around tree and hearth to share gifts and to see one another for a few days. Some spend a lot of time anticipating seeing their families over Christmas only to arrive and begin fretting and anxiously awaiting the moment when they can make the return trip. Of course, the idea of a family Christmas has its downside. It is the notion of a family Christmas that causes so many people pain and depression this time of year. Some mourn the families they have lost to death and disease. Some obsess about the dysfunctional families they have but wish they did not have. Some grieve for

families they have never known and institutional childhoods where they have experienced neglect, abuse, and pain. For many, the idea of a family Christmas is precisely what they hate about the season because it reminds them of what they do not have, namely, a place where they belong, where they are loved and accepted. For them, Christmas serves only as an irksome reminder that they do not have a place where they can grow and receive support, encouragement, and identity.

Isaiah speaks to prospective pilgrims of ancient Israel and contemporary society. What about those with weak hands that are unable to be about God's work in the world? Those hands will be strengthened. What about the others over there who have feeble knees that act up every time they try to walk just a few steps along the road of discipleship? Their knees will be made firm. What about the fearful of heart, those too scared to trust or to make a leap of faith, too scared to step out of the familiar and into an unknown future merely on a word and a promise? To all such persons wandering around without hope or joy, Isaiah speaks boldly and with conviction: "Be strong, do not fear! / Here is your God. / ... He will come and save you" (verse 4).

For those who have ears to hear, this text describes more than a holiday vacation or an Adventure across interesting landscape. Isaiah describes a life journey, a way home, our true home in God, a path of holiness where God's faithful can grow in grace, love, and service. "And the ransomed of the LORD shall return" (verse 10). *Ransomed* is a biblical word that evokes images of a people bought with a price; delivered from captors; and set free to live, to love, and to walk in freedom. It is an Advent invitation to embark on a different kind of journey, a pilgrimage of discipleship, a lifelong pursuit of a holiness into the very heart of God where "no traveler, not even fools, shall go astray" (verse 8).

What images come to mind when you think of home? In what ways are such images transformed or expanded when you consider life in God your true home?

What does it mean to say that God is the beginning, middle, and end of your life's journey?

CULTIVATING PATIENCE
JAMES 5:7-10

Though patience is listed as one of the fruit of the Spirit (Galatians 5:22), it often gets a bad rap. For years my wife has told her family and close friends that they should never pray for patience. Her rationale? It is one of those prayers that God never fails to answer and answer swiftly. She is convinced that if one prays for patience, God will send adversity and hardship so that this important fruit can be cultivated, grow, and flourish.

I have to admit that patience is not my strongest suit either. Every time I reflect on Christian patience, I am reminded of a childhood tune that I heard repeatedly over the years. The tape my mother used to play sounded like the chipmunks on a heavy dose of caffeine. The first line said, "I can't wait to have patience," which points to the irony of acquiring and practicing this Christian virtue. Patience comes slowly, and it is counter to the culture around us that wants everything yesterday.

The season of Advent contains its own summons to be patient. While the rest of the world starts celebrating aspects of Christmas the day after Thanksgiving, the church suggests that Christians should cease and desist from all the rushing around. Though many people cannot wait to begin singing all the Christmas carols in late November, some churches choose to sing their way through with Advent hymns and songs such as "O Come, O Come Emmanuel" and "Come Thou Long Expected Jesus." Many of us deck the halls with greenery and our lawns with hundreds of lights several weeks before the 25th. At the same time, we witness the gradual light of the Advent wreath that grows steadily each of the four Sundays of Advent in anticipation of the true Light of the world. While some of us close up the Christmas shop on the 26th by dumping our trees at the curb and pushing out the trash cart full of boxes and discarded paper, others of us are just getting started with Christmas as we celebrate the full 12 days of the feast that ends with the ancient celebration of the Epiphany on January 6th.

This liturgical "pacing" of the beginning weeks of the Christian year certainly has its advantages. There is good reason for the church to observe time differently from the secular calendar that is market-driven and consumer-oriented. Yet the exhortation in James to "be patient" is about much more than slowing down or waiting to sing carols. The admonition issued in this short epistle is given to people who are suffering persecution and oppression. It is a word to the down and out. It is a glimmer of hope to those who are despairing. It is a clarion call to persevere despite mistreatment and marginalization.

The verses just prior to this passage lay out the larger context: "Come now, you rich people, weep and wail for the miseries that are coming to you. You have lived on the earth in luxury and in pleasure; you have fattened your hearts in a day of slaughter. You have condemned and murdered the righteous one, who does not resist you" (James 5:1,5-6). With verse 7, the beginning of today's Scripture, James's tone shifts from condemnation to edification: "Be patient, therefore, beloved, until the coming of the Lord.... Do not grumble against one another, so that you may not be judged" (James 5:7, 9).

The patience spoken of here may be more accurately rendered as "long-suffering." Christians suffering economic oppression by the rich are exhorted to persevere and not take matters into their own hands, for the judge is "standing at the doors!" (verse 9). Those who are suffering now are called upon to withhold their grumbling against one another and trust God, who is "compassionate and merciful" (verse 11). The Christian virtue expounded in these short verses in James has less to do with slowing down and taking it easy and more to do with trusting God, waiting on God, and believing that God will come again soon to save, redeem, restore, and renew.

As James indicates in verse 10, the Scriptures are full of exemplars of such patience. The Israelites delivered from Egyptian oppression acquired patience the hard way, voicing their impatience and mistrust so often that eventually God let them stew for a while in the pot they had been cooking; 40 years in the wilderness ought to teach a person something. Hannah waited for years to bear a child and patiently endured the taunts and provocations of her rival, Peninnah (1 Samuel 1). God, exercising divine patience with rebellious humanity, sent many a prophet to warn, exhort, and persuade God's people to return to God, repent of their sins, and wait on the Lord's deliverance. James himself uses Job as an example of patience in verse 11.

The King James Version of James 5:11, "Ye have heard of the patience of Job," is the source of the popular phrase that almost everyone has heard at one time or another: "the patience of Job." It is a line that has always puzzled me. A close reading of the Book of Job reveals that patience in Job's context certainly seems to have a different meaning than how we understand the word. Job is certainly not one to sit quietly in the corner and wait calmly for things to change. He is most certainly not the inspiration for a lot of contemporary dictionary definitions of *patience* that describe it as "even tempered care without complaint."[1] Does Job demonstrate perseverance in the midst of suffering? Yes. Endurance in the presence of inexplicable calamity? Yes. A fervent prayer life in time of trouble? Absolutely, and he also expresses brutally honest complaint, frustration, and desperation. "As for me, is my complaint addressed to mortals? / Why should I not be impatient? / Look at me, and be appalled, / and lay your hand upon your mouth" (Job 21:4-5).

If patience is a Christian virtue, it is not a wimpy, passive, and silent resignation to life as we know it. It is a radical, vocal, trusting, and active waiting on God even when circumstances around us might try to rattle our resolve and shake our faith. James does exhort us to avoid "grumbling against one another," which implies, at the very least, that we need to avoid the finger-pointing blame game.

What James does not say is that such patience requires silent acquiesce to evil, injustice, and oppression. Instead, we are called to persevere in the wilderness for as long as is necessary, here in this land between Egypt and God's promised future before us. Therefore "strengthen your hearts, for the coming of the Lord is near" (James 5:8).

How does a biblical understanding of patience offer help for your life as a Christian?

In what ways does God give you hope during difficult times?

What might you do to cultivate Christian patience?

A DIFFERENT ADVENT PERSPECTIVE
MATTHEW 11:2-11

My youngest daughter used to love storybooks. She would listen to Mom and Dad read for hours at a time. It did not matter who was reading, as long as she was able to sit beside them and listen to the story. One of her favorites was a Berenstain Bears story, one of several books designed to teach children as they learn to read. Her favorite story, *Inside, Outside, Upside Down*, helps children learn about position and location.

Junior (a small bear) is playing at home and gets into an empty cardboard box sitting in the living room. He closes the lid and peeks out through the breathing holes to see what is going on outside. Before you know it, along comes an adult bear with a big hand-truck. He takes the box, flips it over, places it on the hand-truck, and proceeds to wheel it outside and onto a pickup truck. Now Junior is inside the box, outside the house, and upside down in the truck. Peering from inside, Junior begins to see the world from a different perspective. Everything looks different to Junior when he is upside down. Trees look like they are standing on clouds. Grass is growing in the heavens and the sky is under his feet. Eventually the box lands back on the ground and flips back over. Once again, Junior, and the world as he perceived it, is "right-side up."

Sometimes something as simple and innocent as a children's story expands our perceptions of the world. We may be looking at the same trees, the same house, the same grass, the same road; but if we were to adjust our perception just a bit, the whole landscape might reveal new realities, new possibilities, and a whole new way of seeing life. Something like this seems to be going on in the Gospel passage for today and the one who has been flipped over and given an opportunity to see things differently is John the Baptist.

John obviously had certain expectations about the advent of the Messiah. As Jesus points out, John was a prophet (Matthew 11:9). John was old-school; he was steeped in the tradition of the wilderness prophets of ancient Israel. He even dressed like them (2 Kings 1:8; Matthew 3:4). John had a two-pronged expectation similar to many first-century Jews—first, that the Messiah would come again and most likely during his lifetime; and second, that when the Messiah did come, he would rain down judgment on the disobedient and reestablish the righteous of Israel as the Scriptures had foretold. John was, among other things, an avid student of Scripture.

The theme of John's wilderness preaching was "repent, for the kingdom of heaven has come near" (Matthew 3:2). Those who refused to do so might quickly discover just what he meant when he spoke of the "wrath to come" (Matthew 3:7-10). John's sermon in Matthew 3 is full of fiery judgment, wrath, and warning. John was not making any of this judgment stuff up, of course, as any serious student of the Hebrew Scriptures can attest. Judgment and restoration of righteousness is part and parcel of what God is up to in the world, but maybe John misunderstood what the role of the Messiah would be. When the true Messiah actually showed up in person and started to teach, preach, and heal, John's world and John's perceptions were turned inside out and upside down. To grasp fully what is going on in this passage, it is important to remember that earlier in Matthew's Gospel, John had already identified Jesus as the Messiah. Jesus had come to John to be baptized. John initially refused, saying, " 'I need to be baptized by you, and do you come to me?' Jesus answered him, 'Let it be so now; for it is proper for us in this way to fulfill all righteousness' " (Matthew 3:14-15).

So what is going on in Matthew 11? Why is John the Baptist backpedaling? One minute, John is fairly clear that Jesus is the Messiah; but eight short chapters later, he is sending out an investigative team of disciples to do a further background check just to make sure. Now it might be easy for us to assume that John was having second thoughts because he was in prison. If ever there were external circumstances in John's life that could lead him to doubt Jesus' true identity, arrest and imprisonment certainly seem to qualify. Perhaps, however, there is more going on with John than just his current problems. Maybe his perception of the Messiah had been a little different, and he was having trouble adjusting. John had preached about a baptism of fire and Spirit. John had proclaimed a Coming One who would lay axe to root and who would use fruitless trees as fuel for a great messianic bonfire. However, as far as John could tell from the news he was receiving in prison, Jesus' approach was not what was expected.

Verse two states, "When John heard in prison what the Messiah was doing, he sent word by his disciples." The statement begs the question: Just what was John hearing? What news was he receiving in prison that was causing him to question whether Jesus was the Messiah? A quick survey of Matthew's Gospel reveals quite a few things had happened "in between" John's wilderness sermon by the Jordan River and his subsequent imprisonment. In between, Jesus had preached his famous Sermon on the Mount where he taught that people should love their enemies and pray for those who might persecute them (Matthew 5:43-48). In between, Jesus had been busy blessing the meek, the merciful, and the pure in heart; teaching people how to pray, how to fast, how to worry less and praise more, and how to store up treasure in heaven rather than on earth (Matthew 5–7).

Jesus had cleansed a leper, healed a centurion's servant, stilled a storm, healed a paralytic, called his disciples, restored a dead girl to life, and stopped a woman from hemorrhaging (Matthew 8–9). When Jesus was confronted by John's disciples, he did not dismiss them for being insolent. Instead, he invited them to listen, to look, and to testify. He invited them to have their perceptions transformed, carry their observations back to John, and then let him make up his own mind. Rather than dismiss them out of hand, Jesus readily handed over his previous weeks' itinerary: "Tell John what you hear and see: the blind receive their sight, the lame walk, the lepers are cleansed, the deaf hear, the dead are raised, and the poor have good news brought to them. And blessed is anyone who takes no offense at me" (Matthew 11:4-6).

In today's text, Jesus offers a response that has the potential to adjust John's perceptions; and perhaps ours could use a little adjusting as well. It is easy to want to keep Jesus in a box of our own imaginings. We prefer a Jesus that conforms to our preconceived notions, a Jesus that meets our expectations on our terms. This Advent text suggests that at least one corrective for such false per-ceptions is to open our eyes and ears. God's work in Jesus Christ is bigger, wider, deeper, and more amazing than we might have first imagined.

Is it possible that you sometimes have too narrow a view of who Jesus is and what Jesus is doing in the world?

In what ways does Jesus' response to John help you broaden your perceptions?

---

[1] From *Dictionary.com Unabridged* (v 1.1). Based on the Random House Unabridged Dictionary (Random House, Inc., 2006).

The Depths of Deity

Scriptures for Advent: The Fourth Sunday
Isaiah 7:10-16
Romans 1:1-7
Matthew 1:18-25

I have always loved the ocean—its sights, its sounds, and the healing that it offers. There is nothing like a trip to the beach to cure what ails you. The sound of wind and waves takes precedence over the sound of cell phones, over the urgency of e-mail inboxes, and over the stress of rush-hour traffic. The sheer size of the shoreline and the expansiveness of the ocean is a sight to behold, stretching as far off into the distance as the physical eye can go until water meets skyline on the distant horizon. I have always found the ocean a natural place to let go of stress and declutter my thoughts and my daily schedule. It is one of several places where I am regularly overwhelmed by beauty, humbled by my comparative smallness, and reminded that my vision has a tendency to be nearsighted.

As much as I love walking the beach, I also like bodysurfing the waves and playing in the shallows with my family. I was taught at an early age to have deep respect for the ocean. Its beauty is matched ounce for ounce by its danger and potential threat. Along the shoreline, children play, float, and explore the shallows with goggles, hands, plastic scoops, and buckets. They discover and examine all kinds of marvels. Each new discovery magnifies the scope and mystery of the water's secrets. They only hint at the mysterious watery world that lays further off shore in the unexplored depths.

The ocean also reminds me of God. As far as metaphors go, it is not a bad one. Like so many families that travel to the beach, we like to walk the shorelines, stick our toes in the water, and play in the theological shallows where we are still in control of our movements. What might it take for us to set out further into the unexplored depths of God's grace and love? For those who like to be in control of things, it requires risk—pushing away from what we can see and going out into uncharted territory where uncompromising faith and trust are essential.

In our first Scripture passage today, King Ahaz was invited to swim out into deeper water, to place his trust in God and leave the shallows of self-reliance behind. Paul deepens our understanding of Advent and Christmas by connecting the mystery of the incarnation to Jesus' death and resurrection. Matthew tells us the story of two parents who dive head first into the waves of God's will and throw self-concern and self-aggrandizement to the wind. In each case, the mystery and majesty of God's preferred future is spread before us, inviting us to push out from what is known into what one of Charles Wesley's hymns refers to as the "depths of deity."

BABIES AND POLITICS
ISAIAH 7:10-16

The miracle of birth is inexplicable. We try to explain it, but our science and our medical terminology fall short. Even the best of our poetry and prose cannot fully capture the experience of a human being taking that first breath or opening those little eyes for the first time. Books on reproduction can describe conception, pregnancy, and birthing in great detail; but there is still mystery beyond the physiological data. The gift of new life breaking into the world inspires awe and amazement.

I will never forget the birth of my first-born child. My wife labored for over 27 hours; and though she used me as a punching bag during the last half of her labor, I never did garner much sympathy for my role in the process. After hours of excruciating labor, my daughter Sarah was finally born. The nurses quickly took the baby to a warming table where they cleaned her off and wrapped a blanket around her before handing her to me. I was overcome with emotion. I turned on my heels and proceeded to walk out of the hospital room and down the hall, sure that it was now my task to bear the good news (and to bear the newborn babe!) to the waiting and watching world. Before I could fully exit through the door, a nurse gently tapped me on the shoulder and said, "Excuse me, I think the mother might like to see her baby first." I tried to claim temporary insanity for my lapse in judgment, but I later discovered that many people respond to birth in a similar way.

The experience of witnessing new life emerging into the world can be breathtaking, exhausting, exciting, and baffling all at once. It can catch you off guard. It can fill you with expectation, pride, and hope. It can make an optimist out of pessimist, turn a naysayer into a believer, and help those with myopic vision see beyond the harsh realities of today by peeking into the possibilities for tomorrow. After all, who knows what this new person might represent for future generations? Who will this child grow up to be? Will she be a queen? a world leader? an artist? a musician? a farmer? What future hopes, dreams, fears, pain, and joy lie ahead? Who will this child love? Who will she save? Where will she go? What will she do?

The words from Isaiah for this Sunday point to such possibility and hope. The words are full of hope, promise, and possibility—all things that seem to have been in short supply when one examines the circumstances. To understand how dire the situation was, it is important to lay out the larger context of this passage. The first nine verses of Isaiah 7, begin to paint a bleak picture. In the interest of Assyrian national security and commerce, Tiglath-pileser III was busy trying to expand his empire. His goal seemed to be clearing a path to Egypt and the larger Mediterranean seaboard. Any and all countries and kings who got in his way were sure to pay the price.

In an attempt to fight off the Assyrians, King Rezin of Aram (Syria) and King Pekah of Israel joined forces to try and build a coalition to resist the Assyrians. They wanted King Ahaz of Judah to join them; but he refused, so they decided to first join forces and attack Judah. By the time we reach verse 10, Judah is under attack from the north by Aram and Ephraim and from the south by raiding Philistines (2 Chronicles 28:18). Judah was under attack from three sides! If ever there was a time that a king was in between a rock and a hard place, this was it.

It is in the midst of this predicament that we read this dialogue between Yahweh, Ahaz, and the prophet Isaiah. Ahaz was reluctant to ask God for a sign even though God told him to. Despite his resistance in asking for a sign, Isaiah pointed to one. The prophet's finger takes the reader's gaze past the battlefield with the threatening armies, past the anxieties of a king besieged, and past the political realities that threaten all of Judea. Isaiah points all the way into an ancient maternity ward where a pregnant mother is about to give birth: "Look, the young woman is with child and shall bear a son, and shall name him Immanuel" (Isaiah 7:14).

Imagine such a conversation taking place today: Leaders of state are sitting in their seats of power, struggling with an imminent threat; and along comes a religious man with news of a pregnant mother about to give birth. The two things do not seem to be related, but perhaps that is part of the point. Ahaz and all Judah would not be saved by military might or strategic planning. It would not do any good for the king to fire his current administration and try to replace them with new people and fresh ideas. The only hope for Judah is divine intervention symbolized best by this mother about to give birth. One might call it "prophetic insanity," but it is in this sign that God revealed the raw materials for defeating the enemy and turning the world upside down.

It is just like God to take a mother and a baby and plop them down right in the middle of national politics. Ahaz tried to be pious by refusing a sign, but one was given to him anyway. The true question was whether or not Ahaz would heed the sign and trust God or continue with the royal business as usual. Scripture and history teach us that he chose the later. Not content to trust God with deliverance, Ahaz would take matters into his own hands and try personally to engineer a victory by requesting assistance from the Assyrians. It would not bode well for Judah or Ahaz.

The sign given to Ahaz was a mother who would give birth to a child named Immanuel, which means, "God with us." Contemporary ears hear "Immanuel, God with us" so often this time of year that we forget its import. One should never assume that "God with us" means "God is on our side." As the verses following verse 16 point out, "God with us" can mean "God coming with judgment as well as salvation." The presence of the living and holy God is nothing to treat lightly. God's holiness exposes our sin and disobedience. God's light shines in our darkness and illuminates our frailty. God's righteousness stands in stark contrast to our wickedness and rebellion.

Reading Isaiah 7 during Advent reminds Christians that, in the fullness of time, God's presence would be revealed through another pregnant mother in the middle of a national political scene. This time it would be during mandatory tax season under the leadership of a paranoid ruler bent on violence. In the midst of all this political business as usual, God would once again point to a sign; but this time it would be more than just a sign. This time the pregnant mother would be the mother of God and the newborn babe would be Jesus, God incarnate.

Gospel accounts would describe the child as a fulfillment of Isaiah's prophecy: "All this took place to fulfill what had been spoken by the Lord through the prophet. . . . 'And they shall name him Emmanuel,' which means, 'God is with us' " (Matthew 1:22-23). With the advent of this Child, the whole world becomes pregnant with new possibilities for hope, salvation, and new life; but as with the sign given to Ahaz, the coming of God's Son evokes a response. One can choose to repent and believe the good news of God's deliverance given in Jesus, or one can chose to try and engineer their own victory over the forces around them that threaten their lives. Hopefully Ahaz can serve as a vivid example of what not to do.

Have you ever felt as if you were between a rock and a hard place? Did you decide to "let go and let

God," or did you try to engineer your own victory?

HOLIDAY HARMONY
ROMANS 1:1-7

As a child, I remember watching *Sesame Street*, learning my alphabet and watching Cookie Monster eat cookies with as much gusto as I was accustomed to using in my own home. One of the things the show taught children was how to identify things that were similar and things that were different. This same type of question now shows up on exams and aptitude tests. Grouping things together is a common way of teaching the young and the old to identify items, determine their characteristics, and become aware of how they differ and how they are similar. The song I remember invited children to find the thing that did not belong in the group. Many positive reasons exist for putting things in categories. Categories help people develop basic skills in observation and organization.

The only problem with the process of categorization is that such techniques often lead to erroneous conclusions. Just because two things look different and have been placed in different categories for organizational purposes does not mean they do not "belong" together. "Christmas" and "Easter." How is that for a holiday clash? One of these celebrations belongs in the winter, and the other belongs in the spring. Children who know less of the biblical stories than the popularized ones might have their own questions, such as "What does Santa have to do with the Easter bunny?" "What do presents under the Christmas tree have to do with a basket full of plastic grass, eggs, and chocolate?" Even those who may have a little Sunday school learning under their belts might come up with another one: "What does the manger have to do with the empty tomb?"

Now that is an interesting question. It may be similar to the question that ran through your head when you saw this reading from Romans 1 right here in the middle of our fourth Sunday of Advent Scripture passages, just days before Christmas. Why are we reading Paul's letter to Rome today? What relation does this have to the church season we are in? This is an obvious category mistake, and someone needs to be told. Just who serves on that lectionary committee anyway? What in the world were they thinking? They obviously did not grow up watching *Sesame Street*!

I like to imagine Paul walking right into the middle of our fourth Sunday of Advent worship service. In my mind's eye, I hear the conversation going something like this:

Paul: Wow, you guys have really been decorating in here. I like all the colors and everything. By the way, did you notice you have a tree growing inside your building?

Worship Leader: It is not growing through the floor. It is a tree we cut down each year and bring into worship during the Advent and Christmas seasons. How do you like the small Nativity scenes we have? Look. This is Mary. This is Joseph. These are the shepherds who came. Here is the manger where Jesus was laid after he was born. We use these things to tell the whole Christmas story.

Paul: I don't want to burst your bubble or anything; but if you want to tell the "whole story," you have missed the most important part. Christmas means nothing without Easter.

Ok, enough with my imaginary visit from the great missionary of the early church; but I believe reading Romans 1:1-7 on the fourth Sunday of Advent has much the same effect as my make-believe visit from the apostle. Paul's words serve as a vivid reminder that we only know about the birth of Jesus because Jesus died on a cross and rose again on the third day. Mark, the earliest Gospel account of Jesus' life, does not even bother with a birth narrative but begins with Jesus' baptism and adult ministry. It was only after there was an empty tomb that later Christians would become interested in the details of Jesus' birth in Bethlehem.

Paul's letter to Rome begins with what some scholars believe is part of an ancient Christian creed. It is easy to see why one might think so. It even reads like one, especially if you write it own in creedal form:

> *The gospel concerning his Son,*
> *who was descended from David*
> *according to the flesh*
> *and was declared to be Son of God with power*
> *according to the spirit of holiness*
> *by resurrection from the dead,*
> *Jesus Christ our Lord,*
> *through whom we have received grace and apostleship.* (1:3-5)

These words reveal that Christmas and Easter belong together. One cannot be fully comprehended without the other. Each event in Jesus' life interprets and harmonizes with the other. The great hymns "Hark! The Herald Angels Sing" and "Christ the Lord Is Risen Today" share more in common than Charles Wesley's authorship. They do not represent musical or theological cacophony. This is no category mistake, despite what one may have learned from *Sesame Street*.

One might call this passage from Romans Paul's contribution to Advent, his "Christmas Creed" for this year's study and reflection. In it, he proclaims that Jesus was fully human "according to the flesh" and fully God "according to the spirit of holiness." Paul points out that Jesus was a Jewish descendant of David and that his universal message of salvation intended to "bring about obedience of faith among all the Gentiles" (verse 5). He proclaims the good news of Jesus—that he came to earth as God's only Son and that he died and rose again that all might be saved. I like to call that "Holiday Harmony."

What relationship do you see between Christmas and Easter? between Incarnation and Resurrection?

HONORING GOD
BEFORE OURSELVES
MATTHEW 1:18-25

The rumor mill loves scandal. In truth, the rumor mill loves just about any type of personal information, noteworthy or not. My first experience living in a small town quickly taught me this lesson. Things that were said at the local grocery would later be circulated at a Wednesday night supper or at the weekend pig pickin'. If someone was pulled over by the police on Friday night, telephone lines would be burning hot with news come Saturday morning. Picking up the daily newspaper for the county was like going to the library archives to get your information. By the time it went across a legitimate news desk, it was not just news anymore; it was old news.

I do not know if first-century Palestine had anything like our contemporary gossips; but if it did, Matthew's Gospel certainly provided plenty of grist for the mill. I can just imagine it. All the news surrounding Jesus' birth shared in short, urgent whispers that pretended to be discreet, even through the words were loud enough for anyone to hear within a quarter-mile radius. Or maybe it was the other way around. In one sense, Matthew's account of Jesus' birth feels like an attempted clean-up operation, trying to set the town gossips straight by helping them get the story right for once. If so, I hope Matthew had better success then many of us do today. Stopping a rumor mill with the truth is like trying to rein in a team of runaway horses with a "no trespassing" sign—not effective; and if you can get them to stop, it is only after they have already galloped all over the place.

At any rate, Matthew 1:18 does state rather matter-of-factly: "Now the birth of Jesus the Messiah took place in this way." Mary and Joseph were engaged; "but before they lived together, she was found to be with child." Though Matthew's next words, *from the Holy Spirit*, are crucial for understanding who has been conceived and what his presence means for the world, I am not sure that most rumor mills would hear anything after the word *child*. That was fodder enough. A young Jewish girl, pregnant out of wedlock, and all the evidence seems to point to a father other than her betrothed.

The narrative suggests some of the scandalous implications of what had taken place, for we next read about Joseph's compassionate decision to dismiss Mary quietly. Describing Joseph as compassionate or righteous in this instance may strike modern readers as odd unless we remember the context. Jewish custom at the time considered engagement to be as binding as marriage. A dowry had likely already been paid, and two families would have already entered into a binding economic relationship. If Joseph were to issue a private "divorce" from this agreement, he would be dishonoring his family and his name; and he would likely forfeit any chance of recovering his dowry money. Joseph may have been scandalized himself by his fiancée's behavior, but he was still not willing to "expose her to public disgrace" (verse 19). You have got to give it to him, and Matthew does. Joseph was a stand-up kind of guy.

God had other plans for Joseph and Mary, and the stage was set for yet another divine intervention into this couple's life. This time an angel of the Lord appeared to Joseph and confirmed that Mary was pregnant with divinity. In this case, there would be no need for an ultrasound to determine the color of the drapes or the toys for the nursery. Joseph was informed that they would be having a son, he was told what to name the child, and the angel even went so far as to say what their new child had come to do: to "save his people from their sins" (verse 21).

The angel may have been able to set Joseph straight; but unfortunately, no one else in the community received a similar angelic visit complete with a detailed explanation. Joseph put aside his honor in order to honor God and the gift of God's Son. Luke tells us that Mary had already chosen to do the same when she answered the Lord's call by saying "Here I am, the servant of the Lord; let it be with me according to your word" (Luke 1:38). For Mary and Joseph, obedience to God trumped the pursuit of self-interest or any public attempt to save face. It should not surprise us that early in the Gospels, right here in the birth narratives and prior to Jesus' calling of the Twelve, we discover the cost of discipleship in the parental vocations of Joseph and Mary.

In Matthew's Gospel, we get a closer look at Joseph's role. My own kids might read this passage with its attention to sexual detail, particularly information about Mary and Joseph's "marital relations" (Matthew 1:25) or absence of such, and shout, "T.M.I!" (too much information). Though the church (and my kids) may have an aversion to talking about sex, Scripture is far less squeamish about such things. Put simply, God cares what we do with our bodies, including how we use them in relation to other people's bodies.

Read from that angle, Joseph becomes a biblical model of abstinence and self-control. He not only took Mary as his wife after she had already conceived, but he even forfeited marital relations with her until after Jesus' birth. Joseph modeled costly discipleship, putting aside his own honor and expectations in order that God's honor and purposes might be magnified. Not a bad example to use with a generation of contemporary teens convinced they cannot wait to have sex.

Joseph's actions demonstrate what it means to place God's honor above his own honor and desires. Yet the heart of this passage is not about Mary, Joseph, sex, rumors, or public scandal. It is about Jesus. Matthew tells us why all of this took place in this way, and it had nothing to do with abstinence campaigns or model parents. It had everything to do with fulfilling the Scriptures: All of this took place to fulfill what had been spoken by the Lord through the prophet: " 'Look, the virgin shall conceive and bear a son, / and they shall name him Emmanuel,' / which means, 'God is with us' " (Matthew 1:22-23).

"God is with us" in the person of Jesus who comes to save his people from their sins. This is good news to all of us who have sinned and fallen short of the glory of God: from parents who struggle to do the right thing to persons who have used their bodies and their sexuality in ways that fail to honor God. It is because of Jesus that we can be empowered to honor God and, like Mary and Joseph, put aside the impulse to honor ourselves.

How do Mary and Joseph inspire your faith and obedience to God? How do Joseph's actions speak to you about honoring God over your personal needs and desires?

God and Sinners Reconciled

Scriptures for Christmas:
Isaiah 9:2-7
Romans 1:1-7
Matthew 1:18-25

Computers are amazing. I recently discovered a program called Google Earth that connects to the Internet and begins with a digital picture of the earth on the screen. With a few clicks of the mouse, you can zoom in on a country. A few more clicks and you can zoom in on a state, on a city, on a neighborhood, on a street, and eventually, even on a house. The entire program was put together using data and pictures collected by satellites that orbit the earth. It is an amazing thing to start with the globe and slowly zoom in on virtually any location around the world.

Reading Christmas Day Scriptures is like using Google Earth in reverse. Today we start a specific focus on an overcrowded inn, one with a small stable in the back where a birth is taking place. We back up a little further, and we discover all this is happening in a town called Bethlehem, not far from the outskirts of Jerusalem. A few more clicks and we realize that we are in Israel during the time of Roman occupation. A few more clicks and we see the entire globe affected by the events in the city of David; but in this case, there are a few more mouse clicks to go. With an additional click, we begin to cross more than geographical boundaries and see the world before Jesus' time, during Jesus' time, and stretching into the world of future generations to come. What took place in Bethlehem that first Christmas has global implications for all people, at all times, in all nations.

Christmas Day is more than waking early and heading to the presents under the tree. In fact, Christmas Day is more than Christmas Day. The Scripture texts for today all point to what is really at stake in the Christmas story; and it is not something that can be kept behind closed doors, no matter how warm the fire or how friendly the fellowship. This is the story of salvation that has global import and cosmic implications. It is more than just a day in December that comes around once a year.

God has broken into this world in an astounding story of divinity and humanity that boggles the brain even as it transforms the heart. The prophet Isaiah reminds us that this birth brings hope to people who have languished for years in despair and hopelessness. Paul's letter to Titus offers guidelines for how we should live between Jesus' first coming to earth and his anticipated return. Luke's Gospel tells us that if we have ears to hear, in this child, humanity discovers peace, life, and joy.

In the words of the late Samuel Hines, "God has a one-item agenda, listed in one expressive and inclusive word: *reconciliation*.[1] It is a bold statement. It suggests that God's intention, purpose, and desire for the world can be captured in this one word.

Reconciliation implies that a relationship has suffered damage. It indicates division exists where there was once harmony. Such division marks all humanity. Through sin and disobedience, we have separated ourselves from God and from one another. The results have devastated us: war, violence, racism, homophobia, classism, prejudice, jealousy, envy, and strife. Christ came that we might be restored to our original friendship with God and neighbor. It is in Christ, through Christ, and with Christ that the dividing wall of

hostility has been torn down. According to Charles Wesley, reconciliation is also the message of Christmas:

Hark! the herald angels sing,
"Glory to the newborn King;
peace on earth, and mercy
  mild,
God and sinners reconciled!

Jesus came that we might be reconciled to God, and Paul states explicitly that God has called us to share in this ministry of reconciliation. However, there is a word of warning to all would-be reconcilers. True reconciliation is hard work. It takes commitment. It takes unswerving tenacity. The cost to God's only Son was high. We should refuse to settle for cheap imitations. As Curtiss Paul DeYoung puts it, "Cheap reconciliation is unity without responsibility, forgiveness without repentance, equal treatment without restitution, harmony without liberation, conflict resolution without relational healing, peace without God."[2]

FROM TEARS TO JOY
ISAIAH 9:2-7

One of the many sad stories in the short history of the United States of America was the passing of the Indian Removal Act in 1830 and the subsequent forced removal of the Cherokee nation in 1838. General Winfield Scott arrived in New Echota on May 17, 1838 with

7,000 men to round up approximately 17,000 Cherokee men, women, and children. Many would end up dying under the horrible conditions found in the forts and makeshift concentration camps where they were held before they even had a chance to take a single step westward. Another estimated 4,000 would die on the long, thousand-mile trek to Oklahoma. The route that these first Americans traveled was known in Cherokee as *Nunna daul Tsuny*, literally "the trail where they cried." We know it today as the Trail of Tears.

It may seem odd to recount this history in light of the Feast of the Nativity and today's passage from Isaiah, but perhaps that is only because we seldom pay close attention to the context for these verses from the prophet. Just prior to verse 2, Isaiah says, "But there will be no gloom for those who were in anguish. In the former time he brought into contempt the land of Zebulun and the land of Naphtali, but in the latter time he will make glorious the way of the sea, the land beyond the Jordan, Galilee of the nations (Isaiah 9:1).

"The way of the sea" is a phrase that is similar to the "trail of tears." Tiglath-Pileser, the king of Assyria, had conquered the tribal regions of Zebulun and Naphtali around 733-32 B.C. Northern Israel had been forced from their homeland and deported back to Assyria. The path they traveled from their homeland is described by Isaiah as "the way of the sea." Like the

Cherokee, Israel had its own trail of tears, and the people who traveled its path "walked in darkness" and experienced gloom and anguish. What follows in the rest of this passage is a striking contrast to this rather depressing backdrop of forced expulsion and military defeat. God would take this very path, this way of the sea, and make it glorious. God has the power to turn darkness into light, defeat into victory, and a journey of tears into a path of joy and hope. The very road that had become a symbol of the people's pain and oppression is here transformed into a glorious symbol of healing and freedom.

It is a reoccurring theme in the Bible. God has a habit of taking human symbols of suffering and death and transforming them into symbols of light and life. The cross is an obvious example. Today we reverence crosses in worship, hang them on walls, and wear them on chains around our necks. The cross has become the most recognized and widely used symbol of the Christian faith, but it was not always so. The cross was not widely used in worship until several hundred years after Christ.

The reasons should be obvious. Who would want to wear the modern-day equivalent of an electric chair around their neck? The cross was an infamously cruel method of state execution practiced throughout the Roman Empire. It was a horrific way to die. It was used as a public deterrent, most often performed along well-traveled highways, making a spectacle of the condemned and striking fear into all onlookers and nearby travelers. Jesus' life, death, and resurrection changed all of that. The cross, once a universal symbol of torture and death, has now become a universal symbol of life and God's victory over sin and death once and for all.

The prophet Isaiah captured this transformation: The way of tears becomes the road to rejoicing, and it opens the way to the coming of a child. With verse 6, we come upon one of the most well-known and beloved passages in Scripture. For most of us, it is difficult to read this passage without hearing Handel's version of it in our heads. The music itself reflects the shift in the passage from darkness to light as the music shifts from a minor key to a major key with the famous chorus: "For unto us a child is born … / unto us, a Son is given. / … And the government shall be upon his shoulders."

For Israel, these words brought long-awaited good news. God was doing a new thing. A new reign and a new king would be ascending the throne of David. Isaiah predicts a glorious future for King Hezekiah who would later succeed King Ahaz. God's people exhausted by war and subsequent deportation could look forward to a glorious return of a new king of Israel, one who would establish a new reign of peace, righteousness, and justice.

Yet even as these words point to the coming reign of King Hezekiah, they simultaneously point beyond him; to a time in the not-too-distance future when another child would be born in "the fullness of time" (Ephesians 1:10), a child who would establish a new reign of peace, justice, and righteousness once and for all. The words of Handel's "Messiah" take these words from the prophet and lead us in a slow, steady crescendo toward the magnificent coronation names that burst forth in our Christmas Day-worship of Jesus the Christ: "And his name shall be called, Wonderful, Counselor, the Mighty God, the Everlasting Father, the Prince of Peace!"

Handel got it right. It is in Jesus that Isaiah's words find their ultimate fulfillment. This Christmas, God invites us to journey again out of our darkness into God's marvelous light. God invites us to bring with us our brokenness, our pain, and our tears. This Christmas, Isaiah announces that hope is born anew in the midst of impossible odds. The "way of the sea" has been transformed from a trail of tears and oppression into a journey pregnant with new joy and light. Whatever road you have been traveling, no matter how dark or hopeless, it is not the last word on the matter: "The people who walked in darkness / have seen a great light; / those who lived in a land of deep darkness— / on them light has shined" (Isaiah 9:2).

What pain and brokenness have been part of your life's journey? How do you think the gift of God's Son enables such brokenness to be transformed into joy and hope?

DECORATING CHRISTMAS
TEACHING
TITUS 2:11-14

I love walking into the church on Christmas Eve. Most congregations go all out for the great Feast of the Nativity. I will never forget the special Christmas service at my first parish appointment. Area congregations would meet in a small, one-room church building that could trace its origins back a hundred years or more. The church no longer housed an active congregation. It had become an historic site for the rare community meeting or the occasional brief tour for traveling history buffs. It was a chapel that stood empty 364 days a year— empty every day of the year but one during the Christmas season when people would gather for an annual love feast and celebration of Christ's birth.

The gathering was always quite an occasion, and a good deal of preparation was required before the service could take place. Firewood was brought and placed outside the door. The wood stove, the only source of heating, was stoked and prepared for lighting prior to worship. In the weeks prior to the Love Feast, people would continue to bring other items to adorn the sanctuary.

Wreaths were prepared and hung on each of the exterior doors. White candles in decorative brass holders were placed in each windowsill with accompanying greenery, ivy, and red holly berries. Greenery adorned the entrances to the chapel and was hung above the windows and along the walls. A large Chrismon tree, complete with lights and symbols of Christ, was placed tastefully in one corner of the room. White paraments with gold embroidery were beautifully offset by the numerous red poinsettia plants that filled the chancel area and spilled out into the nooks and crannies of worship space. Once the chapel was completely decorated, it was a sight to behold.

Years later, I can still imagine the sights, sounds, and festive decorations for that service. It certainly made a lasting impression. The time for worship was always right after dusk. When congregants began to arrive, they would travel down the small gravel driveway to a church bathed in flickering candle light, light that spilled out through the windows and seemed to dance its way through the trees and across the grass. The church was always packed. I was never sure of where all the people came from, but I always wondered if the sheer sight of such a picturesque country church so beautifully illumined had been enough to get casual passersby to make a quick detour off the highway and drop by impromptu. I like to think it did.

Now that I have painted you a picture, imagine that you are standing there with me as we prepare to hear the Christmas story together. Before we turn to the familiar second chapter of Luke, we first hear this reading from Titus: "For the grace of God has appeared, bringing salvation to all" (2:11). It is one of those passages that begin with a preposition, which suggests that we must go backward in order to go forward. The verses preceding verse 11 offer instructions to older men, older women, younger men, younger women, and slaves. The first ten verses of Chapter 2 all seem to point to one purpose and hope for all who heed Paul's teaching: "So that in everything they may be an ornament to the doctrine of God our Savior" (verse 10).

For those who have ears to hear, this word from Titus suddenly redecorates the church instantaneously, right in the middle of our Christmas worship. The last and most important decorations for our little country chapel are the ornaments that have just arrived: every man, woman, boy, girl, and child. Throughout the Bible, there are numerous images for Christ's holy church. It has been described as the body of Christ, the priesthood of all believers, the glorious bride, and the house built out of living stones. Here Titus suggests another possible metaphor for God's people: living ornaments that beautifully adorn the tree of God's doctrine (verse 9).

It is unfortunate that the word *doctrine* often bears negative connotations. It shouldn't. The Greek word found here comes from the root word *didaskalia*, literally meaning "teaching" or "instruction." Some of the best summaries of church teaching can be found in the church's historic creeds and confessions of faith. The Apostles' Creed and the Nicene Creed are the most widely known and recognized. Both share a trinitarian structure that seek to witness to God's grace in creation; in the life, death, and resurrection of Jesus Christ; and in the ongoing work of the Holy Spirit in the world and in the church until Christ comes again in final victory.

The Nicene Creed is my favorite one for the Christmas season because it captures many of the scriptural themes around Jesus' incarnation. Jesus became human. That is at least part of the great mystery that we celebrate at Christmas. It is part of the "doctrine of God our Savior" that we should adorn with our lives (verse 10).

And just how do we adorn this teaching? How do we serve to beautify God's teachings as living ornaments? Titus breaks it down for us and calls us to "renounce impiety and worldly passions, and in the present age to live lives that are self-controlled, upright, and godly, while we wait for the blessed hope and the manifestation of the glory of our great God and Savior, Jesus Christ" (verses 12-13). If we gave as much attention to adorning the gospel with our holy living and loving as we give to decorating our church buildings at Christmas, we might discover people making detours off the road because they see a way of life so attractive and compelling it is worth checking out.

What memories do you have of preparing for Christmas in your church and in your family?

In what concrete ways can you adorn your life with Jesus' teaching?

NOT DONE IN A CORNER
LUKE 2:1-20

In order to gain historical perspective, someone once asked, "Who was the pastor of the local megachurches during the time when St. Francis of Assisi was preaching to birds and ministering to the poor?" The obvious answer is that no one can remember. What people do remember and retell often is the story of an amazing man born in the 12th century around 1181 or 1182 who would later renounce his wealth, marry "lady poverty," and spend the rest of his life as a friar, traveling from town to town proclaiming, teaching, and serving the poor.

A similar thing might be said about the beloved passage from Luke's Gospel. Who can remember the names of the emperor of Rome and the governor of Syria during the first century? We would all probably not know the answer

to such a question if it were not for the birth of a poor, Jewish peasant whose family had traveled south from Nazareth to pay their taxes in the little town of Bethlehem. Because of Jesus, we can answer the question. A decree went out from Emperor, and the first registration was taken while Quirinius was governor (Luke 2:1-3).

Such details may seem like no more than historical window-dressing, but they actually strike a theme that is repeated over and over again in Luke's Gospel and in his sequel, the Book of Acts. Luke reminds everyone within earshot of the Christmas story that Jesus' birth took place in the world. It happened in real time among real people. Jesus was born amidst the ordinary human backdrop of political leaders with political agendas, people going to work in nearby fields, families seeking shelter for the night, and citizens doing ordinary tasks such as paying taxes, eating, sleeping, and traveling. It is a theme that would be repeated again, near the end of Luke's two-book series, when Paul proclaimed the gospel to Festus, another political leader: "I am certain that none of these things has escaped his notice, for this was not done in a corner" (Acts 26:26).

The event of God's incarnation was certainly not "done in a corner"; but Jesus' birth did take place under circumstances that few messianic believers could have anticipated, even in their wildest imaginations. Luke's birth narrative contains several gospel themes that shock and surprise, and the close reader of Luke soon discovers that the surprises keep coming as Jesus grew, traveled, healed, and taught.

Mary "gave birth to her first-born son and wrapped him in bands of cloth, and laid him in a manger, because there was no place for them in the inn" (Luke 2:7). Jesus would continue to have much in common with the homeless, especially in his adult ministry around Galilee and Judea. As Jesus would later point out, even foxes and birds have better living conditions than the "Son of Man" (9:58). There was no place for Jesus on the night of his birth; and from that point forward, the writing was on the wall. There would be even less room for him in his hometown of Nazareth (4:24), and his final trip to Jerusalem would be ambiguous at best.

The entrance with palm fronds and shouts of "Hosanna" quickly turned to a "dead man walking," complete with crowds jeering; mocking; and crying, "Crucify him." Yet here at the manger, there are hints of hope as well. "Bands of cloth" are suggestive, foreshadowing a time in the not-too-distant future when other bands of cloth would be left behind and with them the power of death and sin's dominion over human hearts and minds (24:12). What Jesus came to do was not in a corner. He came into the world in order to redeem the world.

Do not be afraid were the first words out of the angel's mouth to the band of terrified shepherds, who were all living outdoors, keeping a lookout for predators threatening their herds under the cover of night (2:10). The angels we read about in Scripture stand in contrast to the ones we read and hear about in contemporary society. We may imagine a naïve, well-intentioned angel like Clarence in the movie *It's a Wonderful Life* or the gentle, friendly angels from television shows or movies that depict these creatures stepping into our lives, setting us back on the right path, and mending some of our broken relationships before they leave us with a smile and a handshake. The angels depicted in Scripture are different. They are much more likely to strike fear into people than to strike up a conversation and shoot the breeze.

"Do not be afraid." It was not the first or the last time that God's word to people paralyzed with fear would be "fear not." Here again, we discover a reoccurring theme—the human tendency to respond to the unknown with fear and anxiety and God's desire to meet such human angst with a word of comfort and assurance. The first words of Jesus' birth announcement would be similar to the words he would share with scared fishermen on the high seas and with bereaved and fearful disciples behind closed doors (8:25; 24:36).

Jesus' birth may have taken place in a poor barrio on the

"other side of the railroad tracks" in Bethlehem, but it was certainly not an event that happened in a corner. Everything about God "becoming flesh and dwelling among us" shouts that this miracle took place in the real world among real people with real problems. What never ceases to amaze is that Jesus, even with his birth, is able to transform startled shepherds into powerful evangelists of the good news. They may have first received the news of Jesus' coming with fear and trepidation, but they left the manger boldly making "known what had been told them about this child; and all who heard it were amazed at what the shepherds told them" (2:17-18).

The themes found in Luke's birth narrative are as relevant to us today as they were to those living in the first century. Jesus is still in the business of breaking into our everyday lives with power, glory, and peace. We all live with our own fears and anxieties, personal and social. At times, it seems that today's world knows little else but the politics of fear and the practice of fearmongering. It is the raw material of so much mistrust, inse-curity, war, and global instability that we often fail to see alternatives to business as usual.

God's message to us this Christmas is the same: "Do not be afraid; for see—I am bringing you good news of great joy for all people: to you is born this day in the city of David a Savior, who is the Messiah, the Lord" (verses 10-11). Maybe we should take the shepherds' lead and carry that message out of our own corners to a world that is desperate to hear a word of hope, peace, and good news.

How do you understand the significance of God's Son being born into the real world with real people that have real problems?

How do you respond to a word of peace spoken into a context of fear? In what ways can you join the shepherds in telling the good news of Jesus Christ?

---

[1] From "The Gospel Ministry," by Samuel G. *Hines in How Firm a Foundation,* by Cheryl J. Sanders (Third Street Church of God, 1990); page 74.

[2] From *Reconciliation: Our Greatest Challenge—Our Only Hope,* by Curtiss Paul DeYoung (Judson Press, 1997); page XVIII.